D0209371

THE
100
GREATEST
SALES TIPS
OF ALL TIME

Also edited by
Leslie Pockell and **Adrienne Avila**

The 101 Greatest Business Principles of All Time

Everything I've Learned

The 100 Best Love Poems of All Time

The 100 Best Poems of All Time

The 13 Best Horror Stories of All Time

◆

Only the Best/Sólo lo Mejor

THE
100
GREATEST
SALES TIPS
OF ALL TIME

Edited by
Leslie Pockell
with
Adrienne Avila

WARNER
BUSINESS
BOOKS ™

NEW YORK   BOSTON

Warner Business Books
Warner Books

Time Warner Book Group
1271 Avenue of the Americas, New York, NY 10020
Visit our Web site at www.twbookmark.com

The Warner Business Books logo is a trademark of Warner Books.

Printed in the United States of America

First Edition: February 2006

10 9 8 7 6 5 4 3 2 1

ISBN: 0-446-57853-3
LCCN: 2005927663

Book design and typesetting by Mada Design, Inc.

Everyone lives by selling something.

◆

Robert Louis Stevenson

INTRODUCTION

◆

We are always selling something, all the time. As consequence, millions of words of advice have been written to help people sell better. Among these millions of words, a few stand out for their clarity, their specificity, and their general application not only to opening an account and closing a sale, but to living a useful and successful life. This is because selling is simply one of many forms of persuasion, and without the ability to persuade others to one's point of view, mankind would still remain in a state of savagery far more primitive than the one we actually exist in today. Accordingly, while this book is designed to offer sales professionals a concise guide to the best that has been thought and said about the fundamentals of selling, the wisdom gathered here can be applied to other human endeavors as well.

This book is divided into four parts. The first is **Motivation**, because no one can sell successfully without proper motivation. One might think that the prospect of financial gains would be enough to motivate any potential salesperson, but in fact, as many of those quoted here emphasize, enthusiasm for what you are selling, and for the process of selling itself, is a prerequisite for success in sales.

The second part of the book deals with **Preparation**. No matter how spontaneous a successful sales presentation may be, it can only benefit from study, practice, and a mastery of the techniques involved in convincing someone to buy what you are offering, whether product, service, or point of view.

The largest section of the book deals with **Presenting**. The invaluable advice contained here ranges from philosophy to psychology to the most basic principles of placing your message before a potential customer. Understanding what your customer is looking for (without necessarily even knowing it!) is as important as a firm handshake and steady eye contact.

The final section is **Service**, because no matter how effective the presentation, retaining a customer's trust after a sale is essential if the sales effort is to be judged successful.

The sales tips in this book represent the combined wisdom of some of the greatest sales professionals of all time, together with a sampling of philosophers, poets, and assorted geniuses of all types. We hope that salespeople everywhere find this to be a helpful guide and an inspiring companion.

We would like to thank our Publisher, Jamie Raab, and our editor, Rick Wolff, for their support of this project. We'd also like to thank Rebecca Isenberg for her essential editorial contributions.

Leslie Pockell
Adrienne Avila

CONTENTS

◆

Part 1

Motivation

Believe that you will succeed, and you will.

Dale Carnegie

Obstacles are necessary for success because in selling, as in all careers of importance, victory comes only after many struggles and countless defeats. Yet each struggle, each defeat, sharpens your skills and strengths, your courage and your endurance, your ability and your confidence and thus each obstacle is a comrade-in-arms forcing you to become better . . . or quit. Each rebuff is an opportunity to move forward; turn away from them, avoid them, and you throw away your future.

Og Mandino

The most important thing in life is not to capitalize on your successes—any fool can do that. The really important thing is to profit from your mistakes.

◆

William Bolitho

Motivation is a fire from within. If someone else tries to light that fire under you, chances are it will burn very briefly.

Stephen R. Covey

Find a job you love and you will never have
to work a day in your life.

◆

Confucius

Recently, I heard the top salesperson of an organization make the statement, "I can't endorse this product any longer." A visiting consultant replied, "Then it's time for you to go find a product or service you can endorse." Within one week, the Number 1 salesperson for that organization left the company. Was that the right choice? Yes. When you don't believe in your product or service, you're being dishonest with your prospects and customers when you present the benefits and value of what you sell to them. Talk about internal turmoil! If you don't believe in your product or service, and don't have faith that it will accomplish what you say it will—then "it's time for you to go."

Byron White

I will! I am! I can! I will actualize my dream. I will press ahead. I will settle down and see it through. I will solve the problems. I will pay the price. I will never walk away from my dream until I see my dream walk away: Alert! Alive! Achieved!

Robert Schuller

On any given Monday I am one sale closer
and one idea away from being a millionaire.

Larry D. Turner

You've got to be success minded. You've got to feel that things are coming your way when you're out selling; otherwise, you won't be able to sell anything.

◆

Curtis Carlson

Always bear in mind that our own resolution to succeed is more important than any other one thing.

Abraham Lincoln

The essential element in personal magnetism is a consuming sincerity—an overwhelming faith in the importance of the work one has to do.

Bruce Barton

Being sincere is the easiest part of selling. It's simply a matter of caring about your customer and believing in what you sell. If you don't feel this way, my advice to you is to seek other employment or find a product to sell that you believe in.

Joe Girard

Motivation is the art of getting
people to do what you want them to do
because they want to do it.

◆

Dwight D. Eisenhower

Two shoe salesmen found themselves in a rustic part of Africa. The first salesman wired back to his head office: "There is no prospect of sales. No one here wears shoes!" The other salesman wired: "No one wears shoes here. We can dominate the market. Send all possible stock."

Akio Morita

Fall down seven times. Stand up eight.

◆

Japanese proverb

There are no traffic jams along the extra mile.

Roger Staubach

People buy for their own reasons,
not for yours.

◆

Stephen E. Heiman

I once heard a car salesman say, "I peddle metal." Well, I disagree. To the extent I do "peddle" anything, I sell helpfulness and solutions. That to me is the heart of the sales experience. That's what a good salesperson really does—identifies a need and fills it.

Marion Luna Brem

When you have a passion
for your product, selling is the natural
by-product of sharing the love.

◆

Kae Groshong

A salesman minus enthusiasm is just a clerk.

◆

Harry F. Banks

Sincerity is the biggest part of selling anything, I found out—including salvation. And I was sure that when I was selling Fuller brushes that those were the greatest brushes in the whole world.

Billy Graham

There's nothing greater in the world than when somebody on the team does something good, and everybody gathers around to pat him on the back.

Billy Martin

Your big opportunity may be right where you are now.

◆

Napoleon Hill

Part 2

Preparation

Preparation

One important key to success is
self-confidence. An important key
to self-confidence is preparation.

Arthur Ashe

When you're prepared, you're more
confident. When you have a strategy,
you're more comfortable.

Fred Couples

By failing to prepare, you are preparing to fail.

Benjamin Franklin

We are what we repeatedly do. Excellence, then, is not an act, but a habit.

Aristotle

Let your hook be always cast; in the pool where you least expect it, there will be a fish.

Ovid

Internalize the Golden Rule of sales that says, "All things being equal, people will do business with, and refer business to, those people they know, like, and trust."

Bob Burg

Pack your todays with effort—extra effort.

Thomas J. Watson

Know your product.
See a lot of people.
Ask all to buy.
Use common sense.

Arthur H. "Red" Motley

Many a small thing has been made large by
the right kind of advertising.

◆

Mark Twain

I am the world's worst salesman, therefore, I must make it easy for people to buy.

F. W. Woolworth

The single most important thing you can do for sweaty palms is rehearse. The second most important thing you can do for sweaty palms is rehearse. Guess what the third thing is?

David Peoples

Ralph Waldo Emerson was quoted as saying, if a man can make a better mousetrap than his neighbor, the world will make a beaten path to his door. His actual statement was written in a journal as follows: "If a man has good corn, or wood, or boards, or pigs to sell, or can make better chairs or knives, crucibles or church organs than anybody else, you will find a broad hard-beaten road to his house, though it be in the woods."

The mousetrap quote was written by an ad guy, Elbert Hubbard, who attributed it to Emerson twenty-eight years after Emerson died! Emerson had the great thought, but it took a good copywriter to make it a memorable thought. . . . You may have great products and services, but unless you can communicate well, you're doomed.

Matt Michel

Plan your progress carefully; hour-by-hour, day-by-day, month-by-month. Organized activity and maintained enthusiasm are the wellsprings of your power.

Paul J. Meyer

Don't start your day until you have it
finished on paper first.

Jim Rohn

When leaving a message with a receptionist, ask for a specific time your prospect will be available to speak with you and be sure to call at that time. Learn the receptionist's name, and address him by name every time you call the prospect. Remember to be courteous to everyone you speak to, as each person is a gatekeeper to your prospect.

Ron Coxsom

If you're making telemarketing calls and having trouble getting past the receptionist, then the next time you call that company go up or down one number on the last digit of the general phone number to reach someone else who might be more helpful. Every time I've tried it people other than the receptionist have been more than helpful.

Todd Benadum

There's no magic to it, and you don't need a lot of natural talent. What you need is a disciplined, organized approach to selling. If you have that, you'll outperform the great salesman who doesn't understand the process every time. Selling can definitely be learned.

Steve Bostic

The business handshake is an essential selling technique to make a lasting impression. The first move you make when meeting your prospective client is to put out your hand. There isn't a businessperson anywhere who can't tell you that the good business handshake should be a firm one. Yet time and again people offer a limp hand to the client. To have a good business handshake, position your hand to make complete contact with the other person's hand. Once you've connected, close your thumb over the back of the other person's hand and give a slight squeeze. You'll have the beginning of a strong business relationship.

Lydia Ramsey

In the late 1980s, I was a spectacularly unsuccessful burglar-alarm salesman, consistently ranking dead last in weekly sales. As an avid golfer since grade school, I fared better on the back nine and still competed as a part-time pro. During a 1988 game, I told my partner precisely how I planned to get on the 18th green: hit the ball two hundred yards, curve it forty yards from left to right, and drop it about six feet from the hole. Then I did exactly that. My astonished colleague demanded to know my secret. I said, "I practiced for years. I trained. I had in my mind's eye what I was trying to do." And that's when it hit me: That's how the great salesmen do it. They practice. They train. I realized that if I worked as hard at selling as I did at golf, I'd never look back. And I never have.

Dave Hegan

Every sale has five basic obstacles: no need, no money, no hurry, no desire, no trust.

Zig Ziglar

It's simple: Sell to people who want your product; ignore those who don't. I spent years trying to get people to buy into Macintosh. We were selling a dream of how the world might become a better place. That kind of selling requires a different mind-set from that of trying to meet a quota. Some people got it in thirty seconds. Others didn't get it and never would. It took me a while to learn that you can't convert atheists. You can't sell oil to Arabs, or refrigerators to Eskimos. Don't even try.

Guy Kawasaki

Clean out your prospect funnel. Put your current prospects through a sieve. The biggest mistake salespeople make is they call on the same useless prospects over and over. If you have not been able to get anywhere with a specific group of prospects, move on and find new prospects. Being persistent is good. However, if you are spending too much time on fruitless leads you will just burn out. After a shepherd's herd has eaten all the grass in a specific pasture he knows it's time to move on to a new pasture. If he does not move on his sheep will starve. Move on if you are not getting anywhere with old prospects and come back at a later date.

Larry Duca

You can learn a lot about sales and marketing from studying insects. The two insects I like to watch most are bumblebees and spiders. A bumblebee flies as much as fifty miles from home to pollinate a really choice flower "prospect." Here comes that big bee. There goes that big bee. He really, really racks up the frequent flier miles . . . know what we mean? The spider, on the other hand, puts less emphasis on "direct sales" and relies more on studying the best principles of sales and marketing. He does market research and determines that if he locates his web in an area of high traffic flow, he will snare more than his share of "customers" without having to pack as little as a toothbrush for those tiresome road trips. Strategic marketing beats road selling every time. Who says you can't make a living sitting in one place? Couch potatoes, rejoice . . . but tend to your "netting."

Stan Rosenzweig

When I prepare for a sales presentation, I try to think like my client and like my competitor. I try to pinpoint every objection that either of them could make to my presentation. I write these objections down, and then I figure out a way to respond to each one in three lines or less. I've given these "scripts" to sales reps, who then used them in their presentations. It's staggering how even the most boring sales rep can become a great salesperson simply by learning to convey a few simple points. If you can move a customer so that he or she can't argue against your point, then you've won.

Mark Jarvis

Are you born a good salesperson or is the art of selling a natural skill? I'm not sure I knew the answer myself until I was fortunate enough to meet the greatest salesman who ever lived. It was a fellow named Ben Feldman. You probably haven't heard of him either, but you should have. In 1979, while I was with the New York Life Insurance Company, Ben led the industry in sales. That is, all the insurance companies, not just mine. Actually, it is unfair to say he led the industry—he dominated it. The top nine agents were all fairly close to each other. Ben Feldman tripled the next closest competitor. I had never seen a picture of Ben, but I imagined what he looked like. Outgoing, tall, aggressive, big booming voice. Really, I guess I saw him as a collection of every stereotype I had been led to believe was necessary to be an effective salesperson. One day I had the rare pleasure of meeting this man, and, in a way, he changed my life. Ben Feldman stood about five foot three, somewhat overweight, had hair a little like Larry from the "Three Stooges," and spoke with a heavy lisp. Not quite what I had expected. Within seconds, however, I was drawn to the unique style that Ben Feldman possessed. He had none of the more conventional strengths that we associate with his kind of success, yet he remained true to his style, made what he had his strengths, and was dominant in his field.

It was then and there I learned the most valuable lesson I would ever receive in my life regarding our own personal style: I could not be Ben Feldman; I could, however, focus on his technique or process and continue to ask myself, "How can I do that so it sounds like Rob Jolles? What is my personal style?" Rob's strengths aren't Ben's strengths, but then again, Ben's aren't Rob's either. . . . Can anybody sell? Absolutely! The key is to separate style from technique. . . . In the summer of 1994 Ben Feldman passed away but not without leaving us a few final gifts. . . . He taught us all that if you commit to your own personal style and do not worry about anyone else's strengths or style, you can become as great as you want to be.

Robert L. Jolles

Part 3

Presenting

Speak clearly, if you speak at all; carve every word before you let it fall.

Oliver Wendell Holmes

Remember, your customers don't buy your product. They buy you. If they buy you, they will sell your product for you. I treat my potential customers as I would treat a stranger whom I wanted to be my friend.

Alfred E. Lyon

If I can tell you one thing: Remember that it's not what and how you *sell* something that's important, it's what and how your customer wishes to *buy* that's important."

Freeman Gosden

Sell cheap and tell the truth.

Rose Blumkin

As you travel down life's highway . . .
whatever be your goal, you cannot sell a
doughnut without acknowledging the hole.

Harold J. Shayler

No one can remember more than three points.

Philip Crosby

Customers usually buy on impulse, not logic. They base their buying decision on how they feel about your product or service. Get them excited about using your product or service and you'll increase your sales.

Bob Leduc

The spectator-buyer is meant to envy herself as she will become if she buys the product. She is meant to imagine herself transformed by the product into an object of envy for others, an envy which will then justify her loving herself. One could put this another way: The publicity image steals her love of herself as she is, and offers it back to her for the price of the product.

◆

John Berger

Sell to people who want what you have. Figure out who those people are by asking them. Ask as many questions as you need to see if they are good prospects. Be radically honest. Do not fudge in order to pique people's interest. If there is no obvious match, cut them loose—quickly.

◆

Jacques Werth

If a product isn't selling, I want to get it out of there because it's taking up space that can be devoted to another part of my line that moves. Besides, having a product languish on the shelves doesn't do much for our image.

Norman Melnick

People don't like to be sold,
but they love to buy.

◆

Jeffrey Gitomer

It is most important in this world to be
pushing; it is fatal to seem so.

Benjamin Jowett

The marksman hitteth the target partly by pulling, partly by letting go. The boatsman reacheth the landing partly by pulling, partly by letting go.

Egyptian proverb

Every additional message causes an earlier one to be forgotten. What do you want the audience to hear? Say it clearly and with confidence . . . then shut up.

◆

Adrian Savage

Most people think "selling" is the same as "talking." But the most effective salespeople know that listening is the most important part of their job.

Roy Bartell

When people talk, listen completely. Most people never listen.

◆

Ernest Hemingway

Make sure you have finished speaking before your audience has finished listening.

◆

Dorothy Sarnoff

If you want to eliminate sales resistance, treat your prospects the way you'd like to be treated—as peers.

◆

Gill E. Wagner

Traditional selling is based on the product or service sale, and yet until buyers know how decisions and new purchases will affect their culture they will delay their decisions.

◆

Sharon Drew Morgen

A mediocre salesman tells. A good salesman explains. A superior salesman demonstrates. Great salesmen inspire buyers to see the benefits as their own.

Carolyn Shamis

A smart salesperson listens to
emotions, not facts.

◆

Anonymous

You never give less attention to the female than to the man. Just because she's not buying doesn't mean she can't break the sale.

◆

Victoria Gallegos

If I say it, they can doubt me.
If they say it, it's true.

◆

Tom Hopkins

When people laugh at your jokes, they are involuntarily agreeing with your message.

Jim Richardson

One of the keys needed to sell is entertainment; the more you entertain your prospect the greater your chance of creating a personal contact. This does not mean going to the pub or girly bars. This means during your presentation, being interesting and animated.

◆

David Beacham

At the age of three, we all possessed three important skills to make the sale: persistence, creativity, and the ability to ask one question after another.

Dirk Zeller

"No" never means "No"—it just means "Not now."

Mark Bozzini

Call the bald man "Boy"; make the sage thy toy; greet the youth with solemn face; praise the fat man for his grace.

Helen Rowland

One of the best pieces of advice I ever received was from an old, grizzled salesman who'd seen it all. "Just *sell* the damn thing," he'd say. "Stop trying to be fancy."

John Carlton

The best way to sell to anyone is to tell it like it is—which sounds simple but apparently isn't. For instance, look at the boys in Detroit. I'm always amazed by how they sell cars. Instead of grounding their sales pitch in the benefits of their cars, they talk about lifestyle and being cool—or about limited-slip differential and rack-and-pinion steering. No one knows what those things mean! People know when they're being duped. So the best way to sell to them is not to try to dupe them.

Tom Scott

Imagine you are so sick that the doctor had to make a house call. Then when the doctor walked in your house, he started by telling you that you should buy some pills, an extra shot that was on sale that week, some brand X bandages that would reduce healing time by 57 percent and some life insurance from his brother. . . . I would not ask that doctor to come back, yet many sales reps have a similar approach and wonder why customers don't buy from them.

When giving a sales presentation, identify what the prospect's headache is, what keeps him up at night. Once you have identified at least three problem areas of concern, then show your aspirin (solution) that will take care of that headache.

Martien Eerhart

Only after you've correctly assessed the needs of your prospect do you mention anything about what you're offering. I knew a guy who pitched a mannequin (I'm not kidding)! He was so stuck in his own automated, habitual mode, he never bothered to notice that his prospect wasn't breathing. Don't get caught in this trap. Know whom you're speaking with before figuring out what it is you want to say.

Len Foley

I was eleven years old, selling soap door to door to earn my way to YMCA camp. I'd say, "Hello, my name is Brian Tracy. I'm selling Rosamel beauty soap. Would you like to buy a box?" People would say, "No, don't need it, don't want it, can't afford it," etc. I was very frustrated—until I rephrased my presentation: "I'm selling Rosamel beauty soap, but it's strictly for beautiful women." People who had been completely uninterested would say, "Well, that's not for me. It wouldn't help me. How much is it?" I started selling the soap like hot cakes.

Brian Tracy

Engage your audience by telling stories. Begin the story even before doing introductions and use this to get their attention and take full control. What kind of story should you tell? The best stories are ones that the prospect can relate to. Tell a story about one of your customers who had a big problem and how they solved it by doing business with you. Make the story engaging by describing it in vivid emotional detail—who was affected by the problem, how was it impacting them, how did they feel, and how did the solution change all of this?

Take your feature benefit points and weave them into the story. They will have ten times the impact and will be remembered when delivered this way.

Shamus Brown

Make eye contact, especially when you are
stressing the key reason for the conversation.
Eye contact is a visual handshake; it is the
way you connect nonverbally with the other
person. Don't stare at the person, but
regularly connect with your eyes. When you
look at the person you are saying,
"Pay attention to me."

Stephen Boyd

At its conclusion, a good presentation summarizes the key themes in a way that makes the audience feel like they just got off the Jungle Cruise at Disneyland. They learned some stuff, had an enjoyable ride with a few surprises along the way—and knew exactly where they were when the ride was over.

Jim Endicott

A-B-C. A-always, B-be, C-closing.
Always be closing! Always be closing!!
A-I-D-A. Attention, interest, decision, action.

David Mamet

Part 4

Service

There is tremendous value in being a
resource for your client. If you can
help them to succeed then they are more
likely to help you succeed.

◆

Lee Ann Obringer

Quality isn't something that can be argued into an article or promised into it. It must be put there. If it isn't put there, the finest sales talk in the world won't act as a substitute.

C. G. Campbell

Being on par in terms of price and quality
only gets you into the game.
Service wins the game.

◆

Tony Alessandra

Make a customer, not a sale.

Katherine Barchetti

It is not your customers' job to
remember you. It is your obligation and
responsibility to make sure they don't have
the chance to forget you.

Patricia Frip

Neglected customers never buy;
they just fade away.

Elmer G. Leterman

The customer is God.

Japanese proverb

The only way to know how customers see your business is to look at it through their eyes.

Daniel R. Scroggin

To satisfy our customers' needs,
we'll give them what they want,
not what we want to give them.

Steve James

Here is a simple but powerful rule—always give people more than what they expect to get.

Nelson Boswell

Rule #1: The customer is always right!
Rule #2: If the customer is wrong,
reread Rule #1.

Stew Leonard

Sell practical, tested merchandise
at a reasonable profit, treat your customers
like human beings—and they will
always come back.

L. L. Bean

Losers make promises they often break.
Winners make commitments they always keep.

Denis Waitley

Always serve too much hot fudge sauce on hot fudge sundaes. It makes people overjoyed, and puts them in your debt.

Judith Olney

Always do more than is required of you.

◆

George S. Patton